THE GOLD GUIDES

STOCKHOLM
AND ITS SURROUNDINGS

NEW AND COMPLETE GUIDE
TO THE CITY

BONECHI

Göran Brämming Gallery AB

The Publisher wishes to thank for their kind cooperation:

SLOTTSBODEN
STOCKHOLM

THE ROYAL
GIFT SHOP

VASA
MUSEET

Concept: *Casa Editrice Bonechi* - Series Editor: *Monica Bonechi*
Project: *Monica Bonechi* - Graphics, layout and cover: *Maria Rosanna Malagrinò, Manuela Ranfagni* - Make-up: *Patrizia Fabbri*
Texts: *Patrizia Fabbri* - English translation: *Julia Hanna Weiss*
Editing: *Patrizia Fabbri* - Maps and drawings: *Stefano Benini*

© Copyright by Casa Editrice Bonechi, Via Cairoli 18/b – Florence – Italy
E-mail: bonechi@bonechi.it

Printed in Italy by *Centro Stampa Editoriale Bonechi*, Sesto Fiorentino.

The photographs are the property of the *Casa Editrice Bonechi* Archives
and were taken by: *Marco Bonechi, Monica Bonechi* and *Andrea Fantauzzo* (pages 94-95).
Other contributors: *Atlantide*: page 14, *Corbis/Contrasto*: pages 13, 42; *Ina Agency Press*: pages 3, 26 above, 48 above,
49 centre and below right, 52, 53 above, 56, 57 below, 63, 74 centre, 76 below, 77 below, 78 below, 85 above, 86, 91 above left and centre, 93;
NordicPhotos/IMS Bildbyrå/Mira Bildarkiv: pages 4, 16 above, 22-23, 43, 54-55 below, 84 above, 84-85 below, 89 below, 90 above,
90-91 below, 91 above right.
Photographs pages 82 centre, 91 below right: courtesy of *Ultraforlaget*.

The publisher will be grateful for information concerning the sources of photographs without credits
and will be pleased to acknowledge them in future editions.

ISBN 978-88-476-1751-3
Internet: www.bonechi.com

A 10 9 8 7 6 5 4 3 2 1

INTRODUCTION

Defined as the "city between the waters," the "city between the bridges" or the "city on the islands," Stockholm is an extraordinarily "livable" city, situated amidst the green woods and the blue waters of the canals that divided it among the fourteen islands it has grown to encompass over the centuries. According to tradition, it was founded in the middle of the thirteenth century by Birger Jarl, regent for his son Valdemar, king of Sweden. It was he who built a mighty fortress on the island of Stadsholmen as a defensive outpost to protect the cities of Medieval Sweden. Known throughout history as the Fortress of the Three Crowns, it was the nucleus around which the new city gradually rose, starting from what is quite logically known as Gamla Stan, the Old City. However, it is quite legitimate to believe that an area strategically located at the outlet of Lake Mälaren on the Baltic Sea and, where the main trading routes, so vital to the Viking cities of central-southern Sweden, converged had already been the site of earlier settlements. What is certain, however, is that starting in 1252 its official "date of birth," Stockholm enjoyed ceaseless economic and urban growth, and indissolubly linked its destiny to that of Sweden. So, in 1397 following the severe economic crisis that had afflicted Scandinavia throughout the XIV century, the long struggles for predominace were won by Margaret, queen of Denmark and Norway who thus acquired the crown of Sweden (which included Finland!), Stockholm was the leader in expressing the population's discontent, exasperated by increased taxes that would heavily penalize trade as well. Led by Engelbrekt, the miners of Dalarna rebelled in the XV century, and the regency was assumed by the Sture family. When, however, in 1520 King Christian II of Denmark, known as Christian the Cruel, invaded Sweden, occupied Stockholm, killed the regent Sten Sture in battle and had himself crowned in the cathedral, the winds of rebellion began to blow with renewed and unusual force. Once again, the miners of Dalarna lit the fuse with a rebellion which, in less than one year, drove the hated sovereign and the Danes from Sweden and brought the leader of the rebellion, Gustav Vasa, to the throne as King Gustav I.

He quickly proved to be a wise and clear-sighted ruler who concentrated all his efforts on the economic recovery of Sweden and of his capital, Stockholm. It was thanks to him that the Swedish state recovered a definite and strong national identity and the hereditary monarchy once again became a solid form of government. It was also he who promoted Sweden's conversion to

Stockholm, with her towers and canals, has always been the queen of the Baltic.

Protestantism, and ordered the confiscation of Church property to replenish the state's empty coffers. Such a decisive reorganization of the country and such a determined boost to the economy could not but have positive results. Stockholm flourished again, in business and as a city, slowly but steadily developing to reach its peak under the reigns of Gustav II Adolf (who was firmly convinced of the need to expand Sweden's territory and radically rebuild the capital) and Queen Christina. Before converting to Roman Catholicism and definitively leaving Sweden in 1654, this educated and intelligent queen transformed Stockholm into one of the most admired courts of Europe and the favorite destination of the era's most important intellectuals, artists and men of letters.

However, Stockholm was forced to abdicate its role as cultural capital and not only of Sweden when warlike monarchs ascended the throne. These men, like Karl XII, were capable of passing their lives fighting on the battlefields of most of Europe. All this, along with severe defeats (such as Poltava in 1709 which led to the loss of its domination of the Baltic, the defeat by Russia in 1741 and the loss of Finland) certainly did not help the country or its economy. In fact, aside from a period of peace and a moderate recovery during the first half of the XVIII century, the country would have to wait for the coup d'état that brought Gustav III to the throne in 1772 before it could truly breathe again. This enlightened sovereign was particularly concerned about his country's destiny and image. He was convinced that Sweden's economy could, indeed, flourish again and that Stockholm could regain the position as cultural capital of Europe that it had so gloriously held in the past. Since then Stockholm's fate would not change, its urban expansion would go unhindered, its interest in cultural programs would never cease, not even under new reigning dynasty of the Bernadottes who came to the throne when the Vasa line died out in 1818. A clever alliance with Russia and Prussia against Napoleon brought about the union with Norway that was to last until 1905. This opened a period of peace for both this extraordinary nation and its capital. Progress would be constant without compromising the livability of the environment, respect for life and humanity.

THE ITINERARIES

GAMLA STAN 9

RIDDARHOLMEN 24

HELGEANDSHOLMEN 28

KUNGSHOLMEN 30

NORRMALM 46

GAMLA STAN

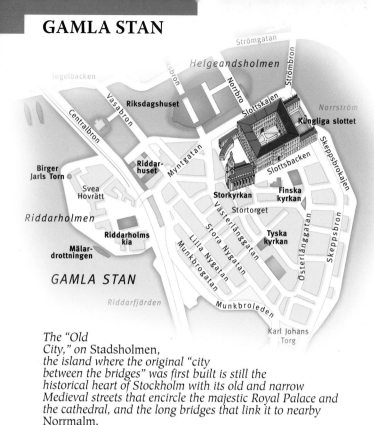

The "Old
City," on Stadsholmen,
the island where the original "city
between the bridges" was first built is still the
historical heart of Stockholm with its old and narrow
Medieval streets that encircle the majestic Royal Palace and
the cathedral, and the long bridges that link it to nearby
Norrmalm.

No matter where you stand, (even "far-off" Södermalm, below, with its curving roads) the urban fabric of Gamla Stan is a closely knit network dotted with slim towers.

The **Gamla Stan**, or Old City, spreads like spokes from *Stortorget*, the Medieval town hall and market place which is brought to life every year in the picturesque *Christmas Market*, a five-hundred year tradition. In 1520, however, the square was the scene of a horrible event that went down in history as the **Stockholm Bloodbath**. Eighty two nobles (including the father of the future king Gustav Vasa) who opposed Sweden's annexation to Denmark, were executed by order of King Christian II of Denmark immediately after he was crowned in the nearby cathedral.

Between copper rooftops, narrow streets, austere Medieval houses and elegant seventeenth and eighteenth century

Glimpses of the Stortorget: narrow little streets, colorful facades, distinctive frontons, and below, on the right, the old Stock Exchange building.

buildings (including the neo-classical *Börshuset,* the former stock exchange which is now home of the **Swedish Academy**), are the surrounding streets, throbbing with life and dotted with cafés and interesting shops. Here it is simply delightful to sit on a bench and savor life in the heart of Stockholm. But when we talk about the lavish palaces that confirm the splendor of Sweden in the XVII and XVIII centuries we cannot overlook the *Gamla Stan,* on the western shore, just opposite *Riddarholmen,*

The city's streets

When Stockholm was a flourishing port and a major trading center in close contact with the Hanseatic cities, the streets of *Gamla Stan* bustled with sailors, workers and stevedores, loyal clients of the hundreds of taverns that literally made fortunes. All this activity enlivened the two main (and oldest) streets in the district, *Österlånggatan* and *Västerlånggatan* which run towards the cathedral and the palace. Originally the first streets that marked a rudimentary urban layout around the fortress, today they abound with glittering store windows, cafés and restaurants.

AXEL OXENSTIERNA

Just opposite the House of the Knights is the statue of one of the most important men in XVII century Swedish history. A shrewd statesman, Axel Oxenstierna was born in Uppsala in 1583 and as chancellor he led Sweden of young Queen Christina in the war against Denmark (1643-1645). He then conducted the negotiations for the Peace of Westphalia (1648) which made the country the greatest power in the Baltic region. He died in Stockholm in 1654.

the elegant **House of the Knights**, built between 1640 and 1674 to plans by the architects Simon and Jean de la Vallée in a flowery Dutch baroque style. The eighteenth century façade is the fruit of the creative talents of Heinrich Wilhelm and Joost Vinckboons of Holland. For a long time this was the Swedish nobility's favored gathering place as proved by the more than 2000 coats of arms of Sweden's most important noble families that decorate the rooms.

For many long years, the elegant House of the Knights was a favorite gathering place for the Swedish nobility.

The Royal Family of Sweden: King Carl XVI Gustaf and Queen Silvia, with the Crown Princess Victoria, during an official occasion with Queen Paola of Belgium and Queen Fabiola, widow of King Baudouin II.

THE ROYAL FAMILY

The Bernadotte dynasty that currently reigns in Sweden has its roots in southern France. It was Jean-Baptiste Bernadotte, son of Henry, the procurator of Pau who brought the family to glory, First as a general and then marshal of the French Empire under Napoleon and ambassador to Vienna in 1798 he earned the respect of the Swedes when, as governor of the Hanseatic cities (1807-1808) he showed great humanity towards the Scandinavian prisoners along with obvious talents as a administrator. And so, Karl XIII who was childless, with the consent of Parliament, designated Jean-Baptiste Bernadotte as the perfect heir apparent to the throne. In 1818 he was crowned Karl XIV Johan, king of Sweden and Norway. His descendant, Carl XVI Gustaf has been on the throne since 1973, with his wife, Queen Silvia who has given him three wonderful children, Crown Princess Victoria, heir to the throne, Prince Carl Philip and Princess Madeleine.

The royal family, is well-loved by the subjects, both for the democratic modernity it has nurtured while respecting traditions and for its image of tranquil harmony. The members of the family live in the splendid Drottningholm Palace, even though the king and queen discharge their many official duties in the huge rooms of the Royal Palace in Gamla Stan.

of today's cathedral with its gothic interior that dates from the fourteenth century reconstruction. The Baroque *facade* was built in the mid-eighteenth century by J. E. Carlberg to harmonize with the nearby Royal Palace. He also designed the *bell tower* (1743) the most visible feature of this cathedral that is squeezed between the houses of the old city center. The site of all official celebrations, the cathedral houses priceless treasures: from the *Silver Altar* (1650 ca.) to the *Royal Thrones,* designed by Nicodemus Tessin the Younger in 1684, to the *Pulpit* carved by Burchardt Precht in 1705, to the oldest (XVI century) view of Stockholm, the famous *Vädersolstavlan* painting. The most outstanding of all, however, is to the left of the altar: *Saint George and the Dragon,* a sculptural group in oak wood and elk-horn carved by Berndt Notke between 1483 and 1489 commissioned by the regent Sten Sture who saved Stockholm from the eager and voracious expansion of the Danes.

Storkyrkan (Cathedral)

Near *Stortorget* stands the **cathedral**, on the highest point of *Stadsholmen* where Birger Jarl wanted Stockholm to have its church. Destroyed by a fire, it was replaced by a majestic basilica dedicated to Saint Nicholas and consecrated in 1306. This was the ancestor

The bell tower of Stockholm's majestic cathedral soars above the narrow city streets. Below, the sculptural group of Saint George and the Dragon, *in the cathedral.*

Kungliga Slottet (Royal Palace)

Just opposite the cathedral, with the *obelisk* raised by Louis Jean Desprez in 1799 as proof of royal gratitude to the citizens for their support during Gustav III's war against Russia, is the enormous *Slottsbacken*. It extends towards the waters of the *Strömmen*, in front of the southern façade of the **Royal Palace**. Here, in the middle of the thirteenth century Birger Jarl erected a mighty stronghold, the *Fortress of the Three Crowns*, which is encircled by massive curtain walls, and that served as the royal residence for years until 1697 when it was destroyed by fire. The royal family then moved to the *Wrangelska Palatset* on the island *Riddarholmen*, while Hedvig Eleonora commissioned Nicodemus Tessin the Younger to build a new palace, befitting a European capital, over the ruins of the fortress. The models were the great Italian palazzos, the style baroque and the objective a well-proportioned, symmetrical building around a large inner courtyard, with harmony of shape and a linear structure. The result was the splendid Royal Palace, one of the largest in all Europe with over 600 rooms, that is still used for its original purpose. It was completed by Tessin's son, Karl Gustav with the help of Carl Hårleman. The palace was inaugurated by King Adolf Fredrik, and it was decorated by the lead-

The elegant southern façade of the Royal Palace dominates the Slottsbacken; in the background the obelisk and the cathedral. Above, one of the solemn-looking lions that guard the entrance to the palace.

The stately western façade of the Royal Palace overlooks the semicircular courtyard.

ing European artists of the period. The triumphal arch on the *southern façade* leads to the wing that hosts the immense *Hall of State* (*Rikssalen*), Hårleman's architectural masterpiece, where we can still admire the splendid chased silver *throne* (1650) made for Queen Christina. This wing also houses the *Royal Chapel* and the *Treasury* (*Skattkammaren*, a sort of crypt beneath the Hall of State) that contains the crown jewels, including the crown that belonged to Erik XIV (1561). In the west wing, overlooking the large semicircular courtyard created by two symmetrical buildings, is the **State Apartments** (*Representationsvåningen*), the oldest part of the palace dating from the end of the seventeenth - early eighteenth century, with

CHANGING OF THE GUARD

A traditional favorite of visitors takes places in the large western courtyard of the Royal Palace. Here every day, to the sounds of the military band, is the spectacular Changing of the Guard Ceremony parade (in summer it also goes through the city streets), in a triumph of sparkling uniforms, beautifully harnessed horses and impeccably timed movements. As to the Royal Guard, it is a militia that has been stationed at the royal residence since 1523 guaranteeing the safety of the king and his entire family.

17

its beautiful furnishings and splendid Gobelin tapestries. In this wing, which is open to the public when royal engagements permit we can admire the *Antechamber of Queen Lovisa Ulrika* in the Bernadotte Apartments (which houses a fine collection of Italian paintings), the rococo style of the **Bernadotte Apartments** and the enormous *Ballroom* (the "White Sea" because of its beautiful white walls). In the *north wing* in the State Apartments is the **Gustav III's State Bedchamber**, where the king died in 1792 following an attempt on his life, the Baroque *Gallery of Karl XI*, one of the most magnificent, and biggest rooms in the entire palace, beneath which stretches the *Bernadotte Gallery* with a rich collection of portraits of the members of the dynasty. And finally, the *eastern portion* of the palace, overlooking the *Logården* extends in two small wings which host the **Gustav III Antikmuseum** (the northern wing) which was opened to the public in 1794 and houses that king's collection of

antique art. He was a great lover of art and architecture and put together a large part of the collection during a trip to Rome in 1783-1784. One of the outstanding pieces is a statue of Endymion.

In the southern wing, is the **Royal Armory** (*Livrustkammaren*), the oldest museum in Sweden, established in 1628 showcasing armor, carriages (including the splendid seventeenth century *Coronation Coach*), weapons, original Swedish clothing and costumes, including the wedding gowns of several queens. However, we must say that

Opposite page: the splendid State Apartments, with the Pillared Hall (above) and the Lovisa Ulrika's Audience Chamber (below).

The lavish Hall of State, with the magnificent silver throne that was built for Queen Christina in the middle of the XVII century.

all the rooms in this extraordinary palace are astounding for their magnificent design and lavish furnishings and decorations. Even the two *grand staircases*, on the east and west, respectively can rightfully be described as spectacular. They were designed by Tessin the Younger and built from Swedish marble and limestone. But when we speak of refinement and Baroque opulence, nothing can compare with the extraordinary, light-filled **Royal Chapel** (*Slottskyrkan*) in the southern wing. This rococo chapel was built by Carl Hårleman to plans by Nicodemus Tessin the Younger. Actually, the old Fortress of the Three Crowns had a chapel: in 1288 King Magnus Ladulås had obtained the pope's permis-

One of the breathtaking staircases built to designs by Nicodemus Tessin the Younger.

TRE KRONOR MUSEUM

The underground chambers in the north wing of the Royal Palace house the interesting *Tre Kronor Museum*. This segment of the ancient fortress escaped the fire precisely because it is underground. Here we practically return to the Middle Ages as we admire the still mighty XIII century defensive walls and the incredible brick arches dating from the 1500 to seventeenth century that enclose the museum rooms. In this historical setting we can view detailed scale models of the Medieval fortress (an example is on the left), and examine the significant modifications that were made over the course of centuries, and specifically in the mid-seventeen hundreds. We can also admire some truly splendid glass and crystal pieces that survived the fire, or were found over following centuries. An interesting reconstruction of the building of the new royal palace provides an overview of the entire history of this nearly thousand-year old fortress.

sion to build it. Destroyed by the fire that demolished the fortress, it was rebuilt and consecrated on 8 December 1754, that is the day after the royal family returned to the completed palace. It was during that period that the interior of the chapel was finished, with its stupendous decorations that employed the efforts of many artists. The *baroque pulpit* and grand rococo *organ* were restored at the end of the twentieth century. It is in this spectacular and solemn chapel – which is open to the public – that even today the entire royal family usually attends religious services.

A spectacular shot of the luminous Royal Chapel, consecrated in the middle of the XVIII century.

RIDDARHOLMEN

Extending towards Lake Mälaren, this small island is firmly linked to Stadsholmen and the historic Old City, Gamla Stan. And what was once the "Island of the Nobility" still vaunts the glories of its past in the fine buildings.

Bathed by the waters of the Riddarfjärden, the embarcaderos along the Riddarholmen are decorated with interesting sculptures such as (below) the granite Solbågen by Christer Berg (1966). Opposite page, a view of the island with the Birger Jarls Torn in the foreground.

SWEDEN'S TROUBADOR

The *Riddarholm Terrass* that faces west (and the City Hall) was named for Evert Taube (1890-1976). The terrace is graced

with a statue of this modern-day bard, author of popular songs and ballads, whom the Swedes consider one of their national poets.

Viewed from *Riddarfjärden*, this island appears to be a tight sequence of buildings. Here, in the perfection of its XVII century urban fabric (with its brightly colored old houses that sport picturesque frontons) are the remains of the fortifications built by Gustav Vasa in the XVI century to protect the **Riddarholmen**. With its visibility and striking cylindrical shape one of these

old bastions, the **Birger Jarls Torn** has become the symbol of the island.

Dotted by sumptuous aristocratic palaces which, for centuries were the homes of the local noble families, the "Island of the Nobility," is very quiet. Oddly enough there are no stores and it is encircled by large embarcaderos offering a view of *Norrmalm, Kungsholmen* and *Södermalm*.

It was built up around the site where, at the dawn of the fourteenth century, Magnus Ladulås had built a Franciscan monastery. Its most precious jewel, the **Riddarholmen Church** (*Riddarholmskyrkan*) is resplendent even today. The unmistakable, soaring, bell tower with its pointed spire was built to re-

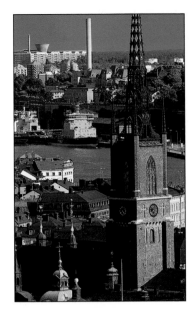

The Riddarholmen Church is visible from anywhere in the city thanks to the distinctive tower that soars above the apse chapels.

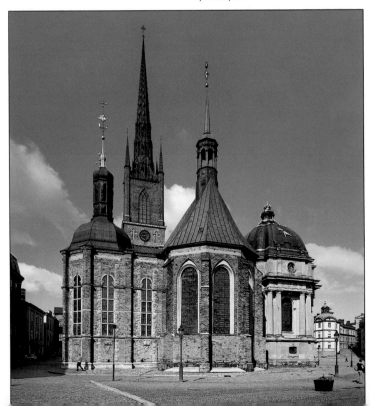

Adjacent to the Riddarholmen Church is the Birger Jarls Torg, a plaza dominated by charming houses and the statue of the city's founder, Birger Jarl. Below, the old houses in nearby Gamla Stan seen from the eastern shore of Riddarholmen.

place the earlier one that had been destroyed by a fire in 1835. Enlarged and remodeled over the course of time the church, which originally had two naves, in keeping with Franciscan architectural traditions, now has three. It is the final resting place of Sweden's sovereigns up to 1950 and Gustav V, whose mortal remains are in the sarchophagi and stately tombs. It is no coincidence that among the many funeral chapels that were added starting in the XVI century, the latest, the *Bernadotteska Gravkoret*, built between 1858 and 1869, serves as the pantheon of the majority of the sovereigns of the current ruling dynasty. Right next to the church is the **Birger Jarls Torg**, a broad plaza with a *statue* in the middle (cast in 1854 by Fogelberg) to honor the city's founder.

HELGEANDSHOLMEN

This, the smallest of the islands around Gamla Stan, *bathed by the waters of the Norrström, and connected to the Stadsholmen by two bridges, is practically identified by a majestic building: the Riksdagshuset (parliament) and the former National Bank.*

The archway leading to the parliament does not conceal the modern superstructures. Below and facing page: the parliament building.

The **Riksdagshuset** dominates the western portion of
Helgeandsholmen. Construction was begun in 1888 to
plans by Aron Johansson and
was completed around 1906,
first housing the two and later
single-chamber parliament.
It was enlarged and updated
several times, as we can see
from the clearly modern ad-
ditions. Today the parliament
building flanks the **Medeltids-
museet** which is devoted to
Medieval Stockholm. The
museum owes its origins to
important items that were un-
earthed beneath the parliament when excavations, to
build an underground parking
facility, were underway. These
finds were so interesting, that
the museum was built instead
of a garage.

KUNGSHOLMEN

Sufficiently far from the historical center and surrounded by water, this large island that extends westward, was long the site of manufacturing activities and inhabited by workers and artisans. Later, when the City Hall was built, followed by other elegant buildings it became a residential district.

Kungsholmen is the home of the City Hall, and it seems to face the entire city. Below, a busy embarcadero.

Kungsholmen, which literally means the "Island of the King", is mainly the island of the City Hall – and more. Here we can visit extraordinary green areas, such as the lush *Kronobergsparken* in the middle of the island and interesting buildings that include the *Kungsholmskyrkan*, a late-seventeenth century church. But, there is no doubt that it is the City Hall with its commanding shape that seems to rise from the waters and perfectly visible from the nearby islands which is the dominant features of the *Kungsholmen* panorama.

Stadshuset
(City Hall)

Stadshuset, the *City Hall*, is an impressive red brick building (eight million bricks), surmounted by a massive tower topped by three graceful gilded crowns, a traditional symbol of Sweden.

The top of the tower (106 meters high) offers a stupendous view of the whole city.

The southern façade of the Stadshuset, an artistic and elaborate blend of decorations and architectural elements, from the columns to the windows, to the small balconies.

Financed by popular subscription and built between 1911 and 1923, designed by Ragnar Östberg, the leader of the national romantic current, the *Stadshuset* (perhaps the most important project in XX century Swedish architecture) was inaugurated in June 1923 as part of the fourth centennial celebrations of the entrance of Gustav Vasa, the first king of Sweden in Stockholm.

The *southern façade,* overlooking the *Riddarfjärden,* with its low portico seems to be "embroidered" by a row of windows, some of which are closed with glazing. It faces a simple, tidy green area that is literally lapped by the water, pruned hedges and *statuary* (mostly by Carl Eldh, but

Above: the moon stop the spires of the City Hall. Below, the terraces and gardens directly overlooking the water.

The statues of Dance *and* Song, *by Carl Eldh add a gentle touch to the balustrades along the City Hall terraces facing Riddarholmen.*

other artists are also represented) that further enhance its appearance. The *terraces* over the water that border the south side boast two interesting sculptures, a female and a male, symbolizing *Dance* and *Song*, respectively. These figures are also the work of Carl Eldh, one of the most prolific twentieth century Swedish sculptors. Along the north-eastern side of the tower there are other statues which attract our attention (*Saint*

Even the Stadshuset gardens are decorated with statues and lush plants and shrubs.

George, the *Princess* and the *Dragon* in a cheerful procession). Made of painted and gilded copper by Gustav Nilsson, during the summer at noon and 6:00 p.m. they seem to come to life as they turn and seem to chase each other in a delightful carillon to the strains of a beautiful Medieval melody. Higher above, there is another *Saint George*, depicted as he slays the dragon. This gilded bronze, by the artist Christian Eriksson, dominates

The stately gilded statue of Birger Jarl is situated in the shade of a majestic baldachin on the eastern side of the tower.

and seems to be protecting the city. On the eastern side of the tower, a stately baldachin frames the *gilded statue* of Stockholm's founder, Birger Jarl, laying on a monumental *sarcophagus*, by Sandberg. Initially, the majestic, quadrilateral *Stadshuset* which almost recalls an old fortress, was designed with two courtyards (according to the typical layout of Italian Renaissance palaces), however, only one remained when construction

BIRGER JARL

A determined and capable statesman, Birger Jarl was first advisor to his brother-in-law, Erik, King of Sweden, and then upon his death in 1250, regent for his son, Valdemar. In fact Birger Jarl, piloted his son's election to the throne. He is known in history for having conquered Finland, developing trade with Lubeck and Hamburg, his efforts to make Sweden the perfect model of western civilization and, above all, for having founded Stockholm — or rather the mighty fortresses on the *Gamla Stan* built to protect to cities of Uppsala and Sigtuna from Estonian invasions and destined to become the first nucleus of the future city.

was completed. The other was covered, and even though it has an airy staircase and portico that still reveal its intended purpose, it now is the splendid *Blå Hallen,* the **Blue Room** with marble floors and red brick walls. Every year on 10 December this room hosts the gala dinner that celebrates the awards of the Nobel Prizes. This room is also the "home" of the biggest *organ* in Europe with 10,000 pipes and 138 registers.

Even the interior of the *Stadshuset* holds other, extraordinary surprises. For example, upstairs, next door to and almost overshadowing the Blue Room as it flanks the balcony is the luminous *Gyllene Salen,* or **Gilded Room.** It was designed as a banquet hall and is decorated with Byzantine-inspired mosaics (the largest mosaics of modern times) by Einar Forseth, made

Splendid decorative elements on the Stockholm City Hall: left, the three crowns, symbol of Sweden and below, St. George killing the Dragon.

The spectacular Blue Room seen from the head of the staircase reveals its original purpose as a courtyard. Below, note at the top the imposing presence of Europe's biggest organ.

HISTORY IN A COLOR

As we admire the majestic walls of the Blue Room which are made of red brick, we ask how did it get its name? The truth is that the original plans called for the walls of this immense room to be done in blue. But when the architect, Östberg saw how finely the bricks had been laid, and their beautiful color, he did not hesitate to change his mind. The name, Blue Room, however, was in all the plans and was used constantly. And so, it was decided to keep the name in spite of the true color of the walls!

of nearly 19 million tiny, gold-leaf covered glass tiles. On the north wall is an imposing picture portraying the *Queen of Lake Mälaren, Stockholm Honored by East and West*.

The **Council Room** with its sumptuous furnishings (the furniture was designed by Carl Malmsten, the upholstery by Maja Sjöström) and the extraordinary ceiling which replicates the roof of an early Viking house astounds with its majesty. However, on the topic of amazing achievements, the singular *Prinsens Galleri*, the Gallery of the Prince, is no less astonishing. It is used for official receptions, but is famous mainly for the lively frescoes of the shores of

The Gilded Room, with the wall mosaic depicting the Queen of Lake Mälaren.

Stockholm with a scenic view of Lake Mälaren, by Prince Eugen, and elegantly framed by paired columns.

Before leaving the Stockholm City Hall we should also stop at the interesting **museum** in the tower. Here we can admire a rich selection of artworks from various periods. The highlights of the museum include casts and original prints of a large number of statues, including the colossal *Saint Erik*, patron saint and protector of Stockholm.

In Stockholm's City Hall, even the ceilings can be a source of amazement, as in the Room of 100 Arches. In fact, there are 100 ceiling arches in this room that leads directly to the Blue Room.

Left, above, the spectacular ceiling in the Council Room was inspired by an early Viking house; below, the Gallery of the Prince with its lively frescoes.

Below, interesting shots of the museum situated in the City Hall tower. On the right, note the cast of the statue of Saint Erik.

THE REALM OF THE NOBEL PRIZES

One of the most traditional and awaited events in Sweden's calm life is the presentation of the Nobel Prizes. In 1895, Alfred Nobel who had been away from his native country for a long time, wrote a will sanctioning the establishment of a foundation which would inherit a significant part of his fortune, and distribute the income "to those who in the preceding year shall have conferred the greatest benefit on mankind." For such an important occasion that required a certain amount of ceremonial solemnity it immediately became necessary to design an appropriately solemn and prestigious setting. Since at the time, Sweden and Norway were united under a single crown, the task was shared by the two countries. Even today, in Stockholm, the King of Sweden presents the prices for physics, chemistry, physiology or medicine, literature; while in Oslo the Nobel Peace Prize is presented by the Chairman of the Norwegian Nobel Committee in the presence of the King of Norway.

Over the years, even the celebrations that were more subdued in the beginning, have become increasingly lavish, transforming the event into a true grand gala. Today, Stockholm offers two of its most prestigious settings for the occasion. The prizes are presented in the elegant *Konserthuset*, and the spectacular banquet for over 1300 guests is held on the evening of 10 December, with the Royal Family in attendance, in the splendid Blue Room in the *Stadshuset* which, because of its size, structure and incomparable beauty is the perfect venue for an event that truly joins history with the social.

The Blue Room in the Stadshuset is the appropriate, stately setting for the gala banquet with the Royal Family, which crowns the Nobel Prize ceremonies.

ALFRED NOBEL

Chemist and industrialist, Alfred Nobel was born in Stockholm in 1833. After studying in St. Petersburg he returned home in 1859 and began to work on the use of nitroglycerin as an explosive; developed the product known as dynamite in a small laboratory in 1863. This marked the beginnings of his huge fortune that was closely tied to the success of dynamite, to the point that his ceaseless work would generate a true industrial empire over the years, and led Nobel to move first to France and then to Sanremo where he died on 10 December 1896.

In his will he made provisions that the immense fortune he accumulated throughout a lifetime of work and satisfaction be almost entirely earmarked for a foundation which, every year, would give five prizes to individuals who had attained international distinction in the arts and sciences.

THE NOBEL PRIZE

The Nobel Prize is given by the foundation established by the last will and testament of Alfred Nobel, who bequeathed a fortune estimated at the time (1896) as 31.5 million Swedish krona. According to the terms of his will, each year the foundation would award five prizes of equal amount (the amount is determined on the basis of the foundation's income, and, it may shared by two or three individuals). The prizes would be given to those who, on an international level (in other words, it was not limited to Scandinavians) had done the most in terms of "services to mankind" in the fields of physics, chemistry, physiology or medicine, literature and peace. This last award, the most complex in political terms and therefore the one which most frequently has not been given, was conceived to honor the work of those who had favored brotherhood among peoples and the withdrawal of permanent armies.

The Nobel Prize quickly became the most prestigious and sought-after prize in the five specific fields. The prizes for physics and chemistry are traditionally given by the Royal Academy of Sciences, Stockholm; medicine and physiology prize is given by the Karolinska Institutet of Stockholm, while the literature prize is given by the Swedish Academy. As to the Nobel Peace Prize, it is the Norwegian Parliament that appoints a committee of five members to evaluate the candidates every year. Starting in 1969 the Bank of Sweden has sponsored another prize in memory of Alfred Nobel: for economics. The first award ceremony was held on 10 December 1901 (the fifth anniversary of Alfred Nobel's death) and since then December has been the Nobel Prize month for Sweden and the whole world.

An exceptional document: the handwritten last will and testament of Alfred Nobel, signed in 1895.

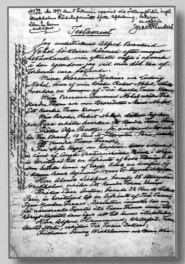
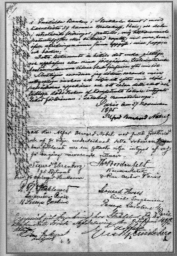

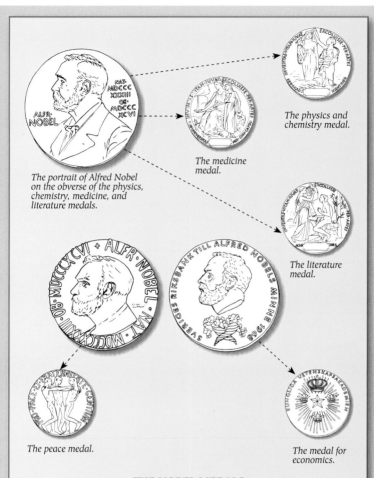

The portrait of Alfred Nobel on the obverse of the physics, chemistry, medicine, and literature medals.

The medicine medal.

The physics and chemistry medal.

The literature medal.

The peace medal.

The medal for economics.

THE NOBEL MEDALS

In addition to a considerable check, Nobel Prize winners also receive a certificate and a medal. On the obverse is a portrait of Alfred Nobel, while on the reverse are images that vary from prize to prize. Nature, symbolized by the goddess Isis rising from clouds, while the Spirit of Science lifts a veil from her face is on the physics and chemistry medals; the Spirit of Medicine, portrayed as a woman drawing water to quench the thirst of a sick child is on the physiology and medicine awards. A youth sitting in the shade of laurel tree while transcribing the song of a muse is the literature award; and three men concluding a pact of brotherhood are on the Peace Prize. Then there is economics prize given by the Bank of Sweden. This medal, too, bears a portrait of Alfred Nobel and on the reverse side the symbol of the Royal Academy of Sciences. The first four medals were designed by Erik Lindberg, the fifth by Gustav Vigeland and the sixth by Gunvor Svensson-Lundkvist.

45

NORRMALM

Situated north of what is today's City of Stockholm this was the first area to which the city began expanding when, in the mid-eighteenth century the confines of Gamla Stan became too tight. It is here that modern, twentieth century architecture has given proof of its vitality and potential.

STOCKHOLM BY BUS

One intrinsically modern yet extraordinarily fascinating way of exploring Stockholm is by the famous *sightseeing buses*. These luxurious coaches dressed in bright, unmistakable colors follow specific routes and travel through the city's streets to reveal its main treasures with the support of excellent descriptions in nine languages.

The traditional starting points are at the *Gustav Adolfs Torg* and along the *Blasieholmen* embarcaderos.

Above, the linear contours of the building which houses the Dansmuseet stand out behind the equestrian monument to Gustav II Adolf. Below, the Opera House in all its grandeur.

Leaving little *Helgeandsholmen* via the *Norrbro* bridge we come to the large *Norrmalm* district. We cross the vast **Gustav Adolfs Torg**, a pretty plaza, designed by Nicodemus Tessin the Younger, with the *statue* of the great King Gustav II Adolf by L'Archevêques. One of the outstanding buildings – because of its essential architectural linearity - skirting the plaza is the **Dansmuseet**, the only institute of its kind in the world: the only museum and research center devoted entirely to dance. Established in Paris in 1931 by the Swedish nobleman, Rolf de Maré, impresario and patron of the dance, founder of the famous *Ballet Suédois* it was opened in Stockholm in 1953 with headquarters in the Opera. Only in 1999 did it move to its independent home. The building offers much

Above, a view of the interior of the Royal Opera House in all its splendor. Below, the statue of King Karl XII that "closes" the southern side of the Kungsträdgården.

more space for the various aspects of the history of dance, from music to documents, from sets to costumes to masks. So, it is no coincidence that the building stands next door to the **Kungliga Operan**, the *Royal Opera House* overlooking the east side of the plaza. Built at the end of the nineteenth century over the site of a theater dating from the reign of Gustav III (it was opened on 30 September 1792) it was designed by Axel Anderberg who wanted it lavishly furnished and decorated on the inside, but created a neo-baroque exterior in perfect visual harmony with its two illustrious neighbors, the Royal Palace and the Parliament building.

Behind the theater is one of the most beautiful green areas. It is a favorite of Stockholm's residents who flock there throughout the year: the **Kungsträdgården** that was created in the XV century. Actually, it is a large park with paths, encircled by trees and graced with flower beds and green lawns. Originally it was a private park and sort of a vegetable garden for the royal family. Later it was transformed into a splendid Renaissance garden by Erik XIV and became a favorite of Queen Christina. Today it hosts festivals, music and dance concerts and street artists. On the south side it is

Shopping streets in Stockholm. Below, a Nordiska Kristall display window.

bounded by the commanding *statue of Karl XII* made by Johan Molin in 1868 to commemorate the 150th anniversary of that warrior king's death. From here, long streets flanked by stores – a favorite shopping destination – go north towards the heart of the city between big, modern buildings. Here we can find *Nordiska Kristall*, a paradise of Swedish glass and *NK* (*Nordiska Kompaniet*), one of the main and best stocked department stores in the city. Continuing north we will have the opportunity to admire the symbols of modern Stockholm: the five unmistakable *skyscrapers*

BETWEEN DESIGN AND TRADITION

Sweden has brilliantly succeeded in combining tradition with modernity to gain international prestige for its crafts and design. The range is vast, from fine glassware to furnishing items, to typical wooden products as charmingly represented by the famous red pony (*Dalahäst*). This carved figure has become a symbol for the entire country.

on the *Sveavägen* that marked the beginning of a new urban development program. After the projects in the 'twenties and 'thirties, by the middle of the twentieth century the program was created to deal with the city's unstoppable growth as the population had surpassed one million and it radically transformed a large part of *Norrmalm*. It was already home to the **Kungsgatan (**one of Stockholm's major business streets, designed in 1915 by Sven Wallander based on models of American streets), which boasts the two oldest skyscrapers in the city, the **Kungstornen** (*Royal Towers*). These twin, 16 storey buildings were erected in 1926 and are familiarly called "Boy" and "Girl." This area is also known for the **Hötorget**, with its colorful fruit and vegetable market, and for the neoclassical **Kon-**

*Left, the Sveavägen skyscrapers.
Below, the twin Kungstornen buildings on Kungsgatan.*

Above, the Konserthuset, with the magnificent Orpheus Fountain *by Carl Milles (1936). Right, and below, the colorful Hötorget market.*

serthuset (*Concert Hall*) that Ivar Tengbom designed, was built between 1923 and 1926 in the style of a Greek temple. This is where the Nobel Prizes are awarded every year. How-

THE SUBWAY:
THE LONGEST MUSEUM IN THE WORLD

It covers more than 100 km of routes, has about one hundred stations and holds a true world record: it is the world's longest museum. From the moment construction work began in the nineteen-forties, the concept was that the *Stockholm Subway* (*Tunnelbana*) should be an unusual venue for displaying the creativity of its main artists, with annual investments of millions of Swedish crowns to embellish it. And so there are sculptures, paintings, frescoes, mosaics, murals and nearly every type of artistic expression by the approximately 130 artists who, year after year, have contributed to this truly extraordinary exhibit. Two examples can say it all: the *Arsenalsgatan* station, near the *Kungsträdgården* recreates a classical setting with statues, columns, paintings and plants, and the famous *T-Centralen* station where garlands of blue leaves decorate the arches.

Solna Centrum.

Fridhemsplan.

The futuristic Sergels Torg, with (below) the sparkling glass fountain, and the unmistakable glass façade of the Kulturhuset.

ever, it is another plaza that can symbolize modern soul of *Norrmalm*: **Sergels Torg**, dedicated to one of Sweden's greatest sculptors (Johan Tobias Sergel, 1740-1814), with a glass *fountain* by Edvin Öhrström (1974). It faces Peter Celsing's (built 1966-1970) **Kulturhuset**, a futuristic cultural center with exhibition rooms, theaters, auditoriums, conference rooms and a very rich library.

BLASIEHOLMEN

Opposite the Royal Palace to the east of the Strömmen, this small peninsula dotted with elegant palazzos, built in the XVII century when Sweden was enjoying a period of great splendor, is a natural bridge to nearby Skeppsholmen.

As we approach this elegant part of Stockholm from *Gamla Stan*, that is separated from *Norrmalm* by the green gardens of the *Kungsträdgården* we clearly realize how its overall, and detailed, appearance – including the contours of individual buildings – can be traced to a major nineteenth century remodeling. It was also during the same period that two of its main attractions the **Grand Hotel** and the **Nationalmuseum** were built. The first, in subdued French-style, was built in 1874 to plans by Axel Kumlien. Remodeled several times, it is the only five-star hotel in all Sweden, and it can host over 800 guests. It is famous for its fine, typically Swedish cuisine and a large room (the *Spegelsalen*, literally the "room of mirrors"), that accurately replicates a similar room in Versailles. Up to 1929 this was were the banquet concluding the Nobel Prize ceremonies was held. The National Museum, home of the country's main art collection, is a beautiful building. It was built in Renaissance style with a vague Venetian air (perhaps inspired by its position directly overlooking the banks of the *Norrström*) by the German architect August Stüler in 1866.

With its elegant buildings, including the majestic Grand Hotel (top) and the National Museum (above), the Blasieholmen peninsula reaches into the waters of the Strömmen between the islands of Gamla Stan and Skeppsholmen.

Nationalmuseum

This important Swedish museum occupying three floors of the large building overlooking the *Norrström* and offers an incredible collection of artworks. In fact, we can admire over 16,000 *paintings* and *sculptures* by the greatest talents in the world, from Bronzino to Veronese, from Tiepolo to Canaletto, from Rembrandt to Rubens, from Van Dyck to Brueghel, from Goya to Ribera, from Delacroix to Renoir, from Monet to Cézanne to Gauguin. These are displayed in the spacious gallery on the second floor. And there are 500,000 *drawings,* as well as the largest collection of *porcelain* in Scandinavia (many pieces are Italian and date from the XV and XVI centuries and are located in the first floor rooms), and an outstanding collection of *tapestries*

Even the building that houses the National Museum is an artistic jewel, as we can see from the staircase, framed by superb architectural details and murals by Carl Larsson.

NATIONALMUSEUM

Above, a luminous image that highlights the harmonious and linear symmetry of the National Museum's façade. Below, the interior where art and beauty reign.

(first floor) from Brussels, Tournai and Oudenarde ranging from the fifteenth to the twentieth century. Modern Swedish design and the *applied arts* are also well represented. Of the countless items of inestimable artistic and historical value we must mention the *coronation cloak worn by Gustav II Adolf,* and a late XV century Italian polychrome relief of a *Deposition.*

On the ground floor of the Nationalmuseum are a large *auditorium* and spacious rooms for temporary exhibits which offer opportunities for discovery and learning.

AN EXPERIENCE FIT FOR A VIKING

For those who want to travel back into history as well as this city's Nordic atmosphere, nothing is better than a tour on the *Old Viking*, a perfect wooden replica of a typical Viking ship. Visitors can sail through Stockholm's waters in a timeless atmosphere accompanied by actor guides wearing costumes and horned helmets and enjoy Viking foods, while seagulls perched fore and aft watch in silence.

STOCKHOLM IN A BALLOON

Colorful hot air balloons floating through the sky are a common sight in Stockholm. They are so plentiful that anyone can give him or herself the thrilling treat of seeing the city from an incredible vantage point, by flying above its rooftops aboard balloons that offer a special service to visitors and lovers of excitement.

From the seventeenth century this small island had been the base of the Swedish Navy as we can see from the many buildings that once served as port sheds and dockyards and the ships anchored along the embarcaderos. Today it is home to the city's main museums.

The "af Chapman," a sailing ship that has been converted into a youth hostel, anchored at Skeppsholmen.

It is no accident that the name *Skeppsholmen* means "Island of the Ships." In fact, for centuries the history of the island (which is connected to *Blasieholmen* by a bridge) and its small southern appendage *Kastellholmen* was linked to ships. This was the home base of the Swedish fleet, site of industrious shipyards where expert carpenters and craftsmen built the famous vessels and tall ships that could cross oceans, true heirs of the great Viking traditions. Even all the buildings were related to the navy, including the austere *Skeppsholmskyrkan* (1647-1650, reconstructed in Empire Style during the first half of the nineteenth century) that was erected as the church of the Admiralty. Today what remains of this illustrious past are mainly the name and a majestic English sailing ship, *"af Chapman,"* an old training ship and almost a modern icon of the island, moored on the western pier and transformed into a youth hostel. At the end of the eighteenth century plans were being made to upgrade the island by planting trees and gradually creating the large city park which is the ideal setting for pleasant, relaxing walks. When, during the

On this page, since 1972 the statues comprising Paradise, *a colored sculptural group by Jean Tinguely and Niki de Saint Phalle (1963) have found their home here, not far from where the Modern Museum would be built.*

The distinctive architecture of the Moderna Museet.
Below, the somber-looking Skeppsholmskyrkan and one of the many
of the island's outdoor artworks, a fine prelude to the museum.

twentieth century, the Navy definitively left its old base, the city grasped the opportunity of transforming it into a cultural center dotted with artistic installations and using the old buildings to house interesting museums. And so we have, the *Östasiatiska Museet*, showcasing ceramics, sculptures and paintings from China, Japan, Korea and India from the Stone Age to the XX century; the *Arkitekturmuseet*, dedicated to the history of Swedish and international architecture with a gallery of highly detailed scale models; the *Fotografiska Museet* with the splendid works of the greatest Swedish and international XX century photographers; and the highlight, the futuristic **Moderna Museet**, designed by the Catalan architect Rafael Moneo in a way that blends perfectly into an urban fabric of scattered, identical low buildings. Opened in 1998 when Stockholm was the European Culture Capital in

61

Boats, ships, piers and embarcaderos: the world around Skeppsholmen.

addition to spectacular panoramic points (even though it is partly underground), this extraordinary museum features a rich collection of works by the major Swedish and international modern artists, as well as photographs, documentaries, books, temporary exhibits, and cinema. And all around, the image of a seafaring world presents itself in the embarcaderos (sometimes skillfully adapted into areas for festivals and cultural events, in the wharves and the low rows of boats that stretch towards the horizon as if to highlight the perimeter of what was once their home.

THE LAND OF CHRISTMAS

Obviously, Stockholm is the perfect setting for Christmas: traditions, atmosphere, splendidly decorated trees, specially-prepared holiday foods (all on the typical *Julbord*, the Christmas buffet with herring, baked ham, roast pork and cold cuts) and then lights, colors, snow and, of course, the enchanting *markets*. This is yet another of Stockholm's great historical traditions: since 1523, and a decree issued by King Gustav Vasa, the goods displayed at these long-awaited markets must be strictly Made in Sweden, (a decisive to centuries of trade dominated by German, Danish and Dutch merchants). And so, the at the Christmas markets of *Stortorget*, *Rosendals Slott* and *Skansen* you can choose from hundreds of items that will make the holiday season unforgettable. Here, the holidays begin on 13 December, which

according to tradition is considered the shortest day of the year, with songs and processions honoring *St. Lucia*, queen of the light, portrayed by a young girl wearing a crown of lit candles.

Songs, foods, decorations and a resplendent Saint Lucia make December a magical month throughout Stockholm.

ÖSTERMALM

Now a modern, residential district in eastern Stockholm, for a long time Östermalm was a rural area with pastures for livestock. Only at the end of the nineteenth century did it become part of the city proper.

Typical views of Östermalm, with the elegant buildings that flank the Strandvägen; above the sparkling white façade of the Dramatiska Teatern.

Crisscrossed by long, wide avenues, such as the elegant *Strandvägen* which flanks the canal leading to the *Djurgårdsbrunnsviken*, **Östermalm** is distinguished by large, stately late-nineteenth and early twentieth century buildings commissioned by the city's wealthiest families of the period. Their majestic façades overlook the many boats anchored in the canal, and some are the headquarters of interesting institutions. One of the

Along the Strandvägen wher Stockholm's leading families built their homes in the late nineteenth century, is still focused on water, with its embarcaderos, boats, ferries and canals pulsing with life.

most noteworthy is the **Kung-liga Dramatiska Teatern** (the Royal Theater of Dramatic Arts) at *Nybroplan*, at the northwest end of *Strandvägen*. It is housed in a typical art deco building, of Viennese inspiration, with a white marble façade and is surmounted by statues created by Carl Milles The theater, which was opened in 1908, is famous for its lav-

THE QUEEN OF THE WATERS

Built where Lake Mälaren meets the waters of the Baltic, Stockholm's life and culture have always had strong ties with water and canals, and the city fathers always succeeded in exploiting these traffic routes. In the city, boats, hydrofoils and ferries are constantly plying the waters and offer the possibility of getting to know Stockholm and its surroundings from an unusual and fascinating perspective. Some of the more enterprising visitors undertake the experience in rowboats or small pedal-boats.

ishly decorated interior as well as its fine performances. All around there is greenery, with large plazas (from the *Östermalmstorg* to the *Karlaplan*) where even the parks (like the *Nobelparken*) overlook the water, and outdoor activities from walking to bicycling to boating are a delight.

However, most important museum in the *Östermalm* district

is the **Historiska Museet**. Dedicated to the Prehistoric, Viking and Medieval periods of these lands, the museum was inaugurated in 1943. Here we can admire one of the richest collections of prehistoric gold and silver jewels as well as unique items and Viking ornaments (which were divided into pieces and used as money), displayed in the magnificent *Gold Room* that was opened to the public in 1994. Many of these precious objects were found during the nineteenth century on farmlands and the owners, admirably, returned them to the Swedish State.

One of the most picturesque attractions of Östermalm is the market, housed in an unusual red-brick building with a slightly Medieval air. Known as the Saluhall, it stands in Östermalmstorg and is known for its wide range of products and specialty foods – and for the unusual elegance of the building itself, erected in the mid-nineteenth century and restored in 1999.

DJURGÅRDEN

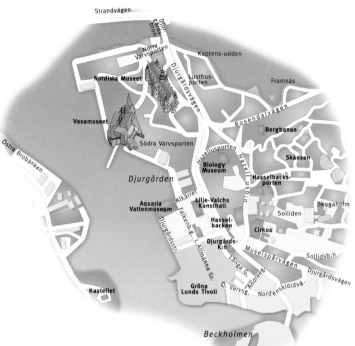

Shortly after 1550 Johan III chose this big, elongated island as the royal hunting reserve. Two centuries later it was transformed into a public park for Stockholm's residents, and even today it is a huge green area at the gates of the city.

The unusual contours of the Vasamuseet dominate the western shore of the island of Djurgården.

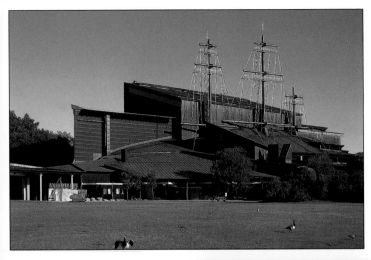

The unique Vasamuseet was built around the salvaged man of war, the Vasa.

The *Djurgården* bridge, opened in 1897 connects the majestic *Strandvägen* to the western tip of the nearby *Djurgården* island, an immense municipal park that is an interesting combination of nature, pleasant entertainment and the home of important cultural institutions. One of the most significant of these is, without a doubt, the extraordinary **Vasamuseet**.

Vasamuseet

For three years, starting in 1625, hundreds of workers, carpenters, cabinet makers, carvers, smiths, rope-makers and laborers worked ceaselessly, using tons of oak to fulfill what was perhaps a somewhat presumptuous dream of King Gustav II Adolf. He wanted a gigantic man of war, the biggest ever, with 50 meter masts, 64 guns and

VASAMUSEET

70

hundreds of gilded, painted statues. All the dockyards of *Skeppsholmen* and shipyards of *Blasieholmen* worked on the project while Europe fearfully followed its progress. The big day arrived on 10 August 1628.

Watched by the curious and admired by the people of Stockholm gathered along the shores of the islands, this marvel of nautical technology, the pride of the king and all Sweden that had cost so

THE SWEDISH FLEET

Gustav II Adolf used to say, "After God, the great protector of the Kingdom is the fleet." This certainty, and the loss of 15 warships during the second decade of the XVII century (including the two flagships "Solen" and "Tigern"), plus the fact that the Thirty Years War was raging on the continent, convinced him of the need to build the "Vasa."

Below, and on the following pages, extraordinary pictures of the "Vasa" and its museum.

VASAMUSEET

much and was to give such satisfaction, could finally be launched. The royal vessel, a mighty warship weighed anchor and set off towards the open sea.

It had gone barely 1300 meters when, just off the *Kastellholmen* shore, as soon as the wind began to fill the sails, it began to list and then, quickly sank with all its guns and a crew of hundreds. The king, who was on the Prussian battlefields, got the disastrous news two weeks later. Was it due to a design error, the ship's lack of stability, the king's excessive pride? In any case, it was a terrible shock. The king ordered a full – and harsh – investigation with many people accused but none found guilty, maybe because it was simply too difficult to attribute the real blame: the king's excessive expectations that could not be disappointed. It was the death of a dream and the birth of a legend.

A legend which after centuries of attempts to raise the ship with its precious cargo, finally surfaced to become reality in 1961. The ship was carefully restored and protected

VASAMUSEET

THE STORY OF A REBIRTH

When, in 1956, the engineer Anders Franzén (who had found the wreck after five years of searching) began to talk about the hypothesis of salvaging the "Vasa" whose hull seemed well preserved thanks to the low salinity of the Baltic Sea, he may not have realized the scope of his idea. The entire country supported the project: individuals competed with donations of money and materials, the Swedish Navy provided ships, equipment and men. Dozens of divers worked for months to go under the ship which was stuck in a wall of mud and clay to lay the cables needed to raise it. Countless repairs and much consolidation work were needed before the Vasa would again see the light of day, on 24 April 1961, after 333 years on the bottom of the sea. Then, it took nearly 20 years of uninterrupted treatments to guarantee its perfect conservation.

74

Whether you look at the scale model (left) or the mighty ship itself, its size, the lavish decorations, the intact beauty of the carvings, and its powerful guns, the feeling is awe, if not fear.

to become a truly extraordinary museum, literally built around the ship with the tall masts protruding majestically from the roof. All the micro-climatic conditions to guarantee the perfect conservation of the ship were carefully prepared.

Every year hundreds of thousands of visitors walk through galleries on the seven floors of the museum to contemplate the 69 meter long "Vasa" from every angle. Replicas and scale models, films and archeological finds tell the story of the ship, the building techniques, the glories of Swedish nautical skill and, of course, how it was raised.

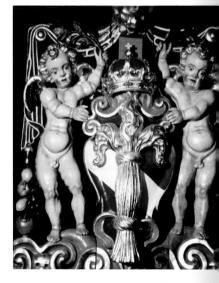

Above, the highly original Renaissance style castle that was built in the late XIX century as the home of the new Nordiska Museet. Below, the gigantic painted and gilded statue of Gustav Vasa, by Carl Milles (1924-1925) stands in the museum lobby.

In addition to the *Vasamuseet*, *Djurgården* has several other fascinating museums such as the **Nordiska Museet**. The museum is housed in a nineteenth century Renaissance-style castle designed by Isak Gustaf Clason. It was ordered by Artur Hazelius who also established the *Skansen*, and started the collections; the museum was opened in 1907. The very popular *Nordiska Museet*, with more than 1.5 million objects on display, its settings (including the famous table set for a lavish seventeenth century banquet), and its galleries offers a detailed overview of Sweden's life, culture, traditions and crafts

NORDISKA MUSEET

One of the most famous buildings of Djurgården which stands out against the unmistakable Nordiska Museet, is the home of the Junibacken.
Below, Astrid Lindgren created unforgettable characters in children's literature, such as the extraordinary Pippi Longstocking.

in the past 500 years. Not far from here, another museum, the *Junibacken* is dedicated to more recent Swedish traditions.

JUNIBACKEN

Perched on the north-west shore of Djurgården, the *Junibacken* is a magical kingdom for children that can be considered a museum of sorts. It was opened in the summer of 1996 and dedicated to the fantastic world of Sweden's great storyteller, Astrid Lindgren (1907-2002). She wrote more than 100 books for children that have been translated into dozens of languages and sold more than 130 million copies worldwide. In the Junibacken, riding aboard the enchanting Fairy Tale Train you will get to know the most famous and lovable characters the author created, from Pippi Longstocking to Emil, just to mention two who are full-fledged members of Swedish – and

not only Swedish! – traditions and loved by "children" of all ages.

77

And this is not all! *Djurgården* has yet another fantastic museum: the **Skansen**. This, the world's oldest outdoor museum was opened in 1891 thanks to the dedicated work of Artur Hazelius. He was an ethnologist who wanted to bring together and reconstruct homes, farms and entire villages from every part of Sweden, complete with inhabitants and animal-plant habitats to show Stockholmers how people live and work in other parts of the country. Today, we can see more than 150 buildings where life is lived strictly according to the historic customs and traditions of the various places. Not too far from here is the **Gröna Lund Tivoli**, Stockholm's historic amusement park that was opened in 1893. Today it is famous, not only for its rides, but also for the gardens, restaurants, cafés, theaters and concert areas.

Opposite page: everything at Skansen speaks of Swedish folk traditions, from the typical homes – inhabited by people who come from those places, to the household objects of their respective regions, to the exhibits that recreate the magical atmosphere of local festivals. On this page, the historic amusement park of Gröna Lund Tivoli, on the western shore of the Djurgården.

GRÖNA LUND TIVOLI

SÖDERMALM

This, the largest of the islands comprising Stockholm, is located along the southern shore of the Riddarfjärden.
It is practically a small city on its own, where old and modern architecture harmonize in a complex area of small plateaus and picturesque rocky shores.

A view of Södermalm, where the Söder Mälarstrand runs along the foot of the picturesque hill dominated by elegant buildings and the Mariaberget's towers.

Above, the modern Katarinahissen; below the elegant home of the Stockholms Stadsmuseum.

The island of *Södermalm* presents itself with a picturesque avenue, the *Söder Mälarstrand*, which runs along the southern side of Lake Mälaren and offers a lovely view of the nearby islands, in particular, *Kungsholmen, Riddarholmen* and *Gamla Stan*. However, the view is even more fascinating from the **Katarinahissen** platform. The elevator, which went into service in 1883 and was modernized several times, rises to a height of 38 meters and offers a 360° view of the city as well as easy access to the just as panoramic *Mosebacke* terrace. *Katarinahissen* dominates one of the island's main squares, *Södermalmstorg* which is not far from the **Stockholms Stadsmuse-**

From Katarinahissen the view reaches to Slussen and beyond to Gamla Stan and the City Hall (above), and to Blasieholmen with the National Museum and Skeppsholmen (below).
However, the old houses are the real pride of Södermalm.

um (the museum dedicated to the city's history) is housed in a beautiful baroque building designed by Nicodemus Tessin the Younger (1680). We reach this plaza via the elaborate **Slussen** bridge

which connects the island to *Gamla Stan*. The bridge was built by using a 1637 weir which served to compensate for the difference in height between Lake Mälaren and Saltsjön Bay. Going further inland we will see other interesting buildings such as the elegant **Katarina kyrka** church with its elegant baroque dome, built by Jean de Vallée. It was completed in 1690 and then beautifully restored after the devastating fire of 1990, and the austere **Södra Teatern**, built on the *Mosebacke Torg* in 1859 to plans by Johan Fredrik Åbom. However, the most fascinating aspect of this island is

Top, Katarina kyrka; above the Södra Teatern and left a view of the typical houses that are now in a protected area to preserve living traces of Stockholm's history.

the maze of streets flanked by old houses, wooden cottages and the charming homes in *Fjällgatan* that take us back to the olden days when, between the seventeenth and nineteenth century, *Södermalm* was thought to be a witches' haven. It was also the seat of severe courts and the site of executions.

83

DROTTNINGHOLMS SLOTT

Sweden too has its "Versailles." It is located on the island of Lovön in Lake Mälaren: since 1981 **Drottningholm Palace** has been the permanent residence of the Royal Family. Built in the XVI century it was razed to the ground by fire. It was only in the mid-seventeenth century, under orders from Hedvig Eleonora, wife of Karl X Gustav that the architects Nicodemus Tessin the Elder and Nicodemus Tessin the Younger constructed the existing palace which is a fine mix of international and Swedish, or Gustavian, Baroque styles, and the French Baroque park. Around the end of the eighteenth century an

English garden surrounded the park which was embellished with a *Chinese Pavilion* and a wooden *Theater* (1766) that still conserves its original structure and decorations. In fact, it may be the only theater in the world that has remained unchanged for 200 years, and that includes its stage machinery, the back-drops and the furnishings. It is for this reason that in 1992 UNESCO declared the theater, as well as the Drottningholm Palace and Chinese Pavilion as "world heritage sites," a designation given to but few places or buildings of particular importance in the history of mankind.

MUSIC, FESTIVALS AND SONG

Stockholm is intrinsically a city of culture, special events, folk and other festivals that are held year in and year out in its large parks. So jazz echoes through *Skansen*, and at the International Jazz & Blues Festivals on *Skeppsholmen*, while the Royal Philharmonic Orchestra offers open-air concerts that delight thousands of classical music lovers.

The colossal, white Globen Arena, the venue for sport, musical and cultural events, is a symbol of modern Stockholm.

GLOBEN ARENA

Going towards the southern part of *Södermalm,* along the *Nynäsvägen,* a broad, and modern avenue, we will have an opportunity to admire the modern symbol of the city, the *Globen Arena.* This is the biggest spherical building in the world: the maximum indoor ceiling height is 85 meters, the diameter 110; the circumference measures 690 meters and its 605,000 cubic meters of volume can accommodate nearly 14,000 spectators. From when it was built (1986-1989) this building with its unmistakable contours has become the ven-

ue of choice for Stockholm's most important cultural, musical and sporting events. Its calendar goes from hockey, and soccer to gymnastics, indoor track and field and riding championship competitions, to circuses, to concerts (for every taste, from Pavarotti to Sinatra to Bruce Springsteen), to events of historic scope (Pope John Paul II spoke here), for more than 100 events each year. An entire neighborhood has grown up around the *Arena,* with stores, hotels, shopping centers and offices of all types.

ISLAND HOPPING

As we have seen, Stockholm is a city that has literally grown from the water. Therefore, it has learned to live with its surroundings which impact all aspects of its life, including transportation which, for the most part is by taxi-boat, water-buses and ferries. Connections among the Archipelago's many islands are maintained

Big and efficient ferries offer daily service between Stockholm and Helsinki as well as other places in the Archipelago; the Viking Line vessels are distinctively red, and the Silja Line ferries are white.

thanks to the ferries as well as smaller vessels and private craft. The largest of these, that carry people and cars are operated by two important companies *Viking Line* and *Silja Line* which also provide daily service to Finland (it is about a 15 hour trip from Stockholm to Helsinki). The *Viking Line* ferries sail from *Stadsgården*, not far from the city center, while the ferries of the *Silja Line* depart from *Värtahamnen*.

SKÄRGÅRDEN

The more than 24,000 islands comprising the Archipelago facing Stockholm, the **Skärgården**, the "garden on the rocks" are favorite destinations for vacations and weekend excursions for many of the city's natives. Easily reached by *ferry* or *taxiboats*, or by land and private craft (one family out of every three in Sweden owns some sort of boat) the islands and islets immediately reveal their rich and varied vegetation and brilliant colors. They are also home to charming towns that have attracted many artists and writers over the centuries.

Views of the Stockholm Archipelago, abounding in rocks, beaches and history, and distinguished by an extraordinary variety of plants and animals, typical houses and enchanting places. Opposite page, center and below, two shots of the Vaxholm area.

August Strindberg used to spend his vacations at **Dalarö**, which is famous for its fishing villages. Carl Larsson and Anders Zorn portrayed the lights and atmosphere of these places in their paintings. Once used to defend Stockholm from enemies arriving by sea, some of these islands still converse traces of their original purpose. At **Vaxholm** – one of the most popular towns of the archipelago – for example, there is still a XVI century fortress which has been transformed into a museum featuring Sweden's military defensive systems over the centuries.

But the greatest attraction, in addition to the beaches and sports facilities, are the old wooden houses. The elegant carvings that decorate the eaves, verandas and windows create a most picturesque effect.

91

MILLESGÅRDEN

Northwest of Stockholm, connected to the mainland by a bridge, the Island of Lidingö is home to the highly original **museum** dedicated to the works of the Swedish sculptor Carl Milles (1875-1955). Set up in the artist's home and park, decorated with Pompeian mosaics and donated to Sweden in 1936, the museum is a rare example of a perfect balance between nature and art. The rooms and panoramic terraces are decorated with many sculptures and fountains by Carl Milles. Several are copies of originals which are on exhibit abroad, mainly in the United States where Milles lived for several years and acquired considerable fame. But this fact, does not diminish the statues' charm – such as the slim figures of the *Musical Angels* balanced on tall columns, the severe *Hand of God,* or the cheerful mythological figures on the *Fountain of Aganippe* on *Olga's Terrace* – named for the artist's beloved wife who did a fine portrait of him. Inside the museum-house we can enjoy Milles's personal collection of approximately 200 ancient Greek and Roman pieces plus items from every era and country. Like the garden, the museum is open all year.

Some of the sculptures by Carl Milles displayed in the garden surrounding the artist's home. Inside, in the Music Room is the organ played by Leopold Mozart, Wolfgang's father, and works by Donatello, Canaletto, Pissarro and Utrillo.

HAGAPARKEN

This extraordinary *natural park* on the west bank of the Brunnsviken Bay, north of Stockholm was created in perfect English style by order of Gustav III at the end of the eighteenth century to become the first urban national park in the world, which is embellished by many pavilions, temples and architectural elements. One of the most outstanding of these, in the northern part, is the ***Koppartälten***, three large copper tents that resemble a military encampment, the **Pavilion of Gustav III**, by Tempelman, but designed, in fact, with the help of the king who had hoped to live there permanently (unfortunately, he died and was unable to realize his dream). Then changing style, as it were, is the **Butterfly House** (*Fjärilshuset*) where, hundreds of these elegant, colorful insects fly freely amidst lush tropical plants, not far from the splendid winter garden, a fine artificial habitat for a large bird colony.

The unusual Koppartälten, literally "Copper Tents," that recreate an old military encampment in the Hagaparken.

SWEDISH FOODS

Swedish foods are quite peculiar because of the typical combination of sweet and savory flavors (it is not unusual to come across meat or fish dishes prepared with salt, sugar, spices, blueberries, cream or honeyed purée), and the ingredients. Here we present a small, but significant selection of traditional favorites from this extraordinary Nordic cuisine.

MARINATED HERRING

For 6 servings: 12 rolled herring fillets/ 2 lemons/ 100 gr (4 oz) sugar/ 1/2 glass water/ 1 teaspoon Jamaican peppercorns/ 1 teaspoon white peppercorns/ 2 bay leaves/ 1 onion/1 leek/ a bunch of dill, that is 6 tablespoons

You can easily find the herring, known as *rollmops*, in glass jars. Start by preparing the marinade. In a saucepan combine the juice of the two lemons, water, sugar and spices. Simmer for a few minutes, taking care not to boil the ingredients. Remove from the stove and let cool. Cut the herring into strips, slice the onion and leek. Rinse the jar the *rollmops* came in: place a layer of onions on the bottom, then a layer leek slices and then the herring, repeat until you have used up all the ingredients. Put the marinade through a strainer and pour the liquid over the other ingredients in jar. Refrigerate over night and enjoy the herring the next day.

GRAVLAX
FRESH MARINATED SALMON

For 8 servings: 1 kg (2 lbs) fresh salmon fillets with the skin/ 3 bunches of dill/ 2 tablespoons sugar/ 2 tablespoons coarse salt.
For the sauce: 1/2 cup finely chopped dill/ 130 gr (5 oz) sugar/ 4 tablespoons (mild) mustard/ 15 tablespoons oil/ 6 tablespoons white wine vinegar

Divide one kilo (2 lbs) of very fresh salmon into two pieces. Place them one next to the other, skin side down and remove all the bones, even the small

ones! Combine the salt and sugar, spread half the mixture over the fish, and sprinkle the dill over only one. Put one fillet on top of the other, so that the meaty sides touch and wrap in transparent film. Put a board and a weight on top of the fish and refrigerate for 48 hours, turning now and then. Remove the fish from the refrigerator, discard the dill.
Sprinkle with freshly chopped dill and then slice the fish thinly, as if it were smoked salmon. For the sauce: combine all the ingredients except for the salt; beat with a wire whisk then taste to see if it really needs any salt, if so add a little. Serve the sauce on the side.

SMÖRGÅSBORD

It is impossible to talk about Scandinavian, and specifically Swedish foods without dealing with the concept of *smörgåsbord* first. Indeed! This is not a dish that can be described with a list of ingredients and serving sizes. In fact, it is a series of dishes that form a buffet which absolutely demands that you follow an important rule: the order in which to taste the foods. Therefore, and it practically goes without saying, you begin with herring prepared in at least a dozen ways, smoked, with mustard, with onions, with curry. Then, right after the herring, the other fish, starting with salmon, then smoked eel, prawns, mackerel marinated in white wine, and mussels in various sauces. After the fish, the *smörgåsbord* offers meats and cold cuts, liver pâté, smoked reindeer meat, the famous Swedish meatballs, and different types of salami, All served with pickled vegetables, salad and hardboiled eggs. Next come the hot dishes like the potato and anchovy *pie*, known as *Janson's temptation*, hot sausages, omelets with different fillings, and fried or scrambled eggs. Next come the cheeses – not many, but very tasty – such as *kryddost* covered with caraway seeds. The bread you serve should be black, or sprinkled with sesame or caraway seeds.

FRESH BERRY TART

For 4-6 servings. For the pastry: 150 gr (6 oz) butter/ 2 eggs/ 150 gr (6 oz) sugar/ 1 sachet baking powder/ 100 gr (4 oz) flour/ 100 gr (4 oz) finely ground almonds.
For the filling: 1/2 pint liter cream/ 2 eggs/ 80 gr (3 oz) sugar/ 1 sachet vanilla sugar/ 1 teaspoon anise seeds/ grated zest of 1 lemon/ 1 basket of blackberries/ 1 basket of raspberries/ 1 basket of blueberries

Prepare the pastry by combining the sugar and butter, add the eggs one at a time, blending well. Add the flour, ground almonds and baking powder. Knead with your hands until you get a very flaky dough. Arrange the dough in a baking dish, keeping the edges thick. In a mixing bowl, combine the cream, lemon, vanilla sugar, the egg yolks, anise seeds and sugar. Beat well until creamy and pour over the pastry. Bake at 180°-200°C (350°-400°F) for 35 minutes. Remove from the oven and cool. Then cover with a layer of nicely arranged berries, refrigerate for 1 hour and then serve, perhaps with a little pitcher of fresh cream on the side.

INDEX